## Dedication

For Alex

## CONTENTS

# Acknowledgements

I am hugely grateful to Alex, my family and friends for all their support and encouragement.

To Deepak Chopra for providing the source of inspiration for a whole section.

To Green Cat Books, for believing in my collections of poetry and offering wise advice.

There are many other people I want to thank for helping me publish this second volume and I trust they will know who they are.

# Foreword By Lisa Davies

Where to begin? Firstly, to acknowledge the great honour bestowed upon me by Sue to write a foreword to this inspirational collection of her heartfelt work.

As I write, I'm trying to recall just how long Sue and I have known one another? It is without doubt many, many years, each of us adopting several different costumes of outer expression of ourselves into the World during that time.

Isn't it interesting how our lives can entwine with one another, walking alongside another; sometimes close, sometimes at a distance? Such has it been with me and Sue.

Be it in our shared love of holistic and natural approaches to wellbeing, meaningful connection with others through WiRE (Women in Rural Enterprise), a love of observing the World around us through our unique creative expression or what has become our jointly held virtual space of the "Abundance and Gratitude Meditation group" on social media.

Little did we know that the World would become a very different one to the one we had always come to rely upon in 2020. It was during this time of "Staying at home" as I personally preferred to describe it, that Sue's first collection of poetry was born.

I was blessed throughout this time, to have Sue share her work as it unfolded, culminating into words captured onto the pages of her first beautiful book, My Words for Living. This was of course, just the beginning!

This second collection is testament to Sue's wonderful ability of capturing what may appear, at first glance, to be ordinary life; magically transcribing simple moments of life's rich tapestry of experiences into the extraordinary through poetry.

So, now it's over to Sue….. and to you, the reader.

I urge you to find yourself a comfortable and cosy space, with perhaps a cup of tea in hand and allow Sue's words to drift from the page, taking you on an inspirational journey of mindful and grateful moments.

Thank you, Sue, for gifting us such a moving insight into the World through your eyes.

Lisa Davies.

*Multi award winning therapist, speaker, trainer, author of 'Get a Life' and good friend.*

# Travel Safely Within

Poems of Appreciation for Love & Life

# Introduction

Even before my first book, My Words for Living, was published in March 2021, I had a large number of poems written, that I felt needed to be seen, read, shared and belong, somewhere.

2021 was very different to 2020, with the New Year celebrations giving us hope for a kinder, more inclusive World. There were, however, some breathtaking highs and some gut wrenching lows. Lots of life's activities were still restricted or unavailable to us, for quite a while. I missed being with my family, at my singing and keep fit groups but did take some UK breaks away.

I continued to channel my abundant energy, thoughts, feelings and observations into words and creating more poems.

Towards the end of the year, 2021, I was still a little wary of really getting 'out there'. Why?

After being so careful looking after our health, exercise, nutrition and bug avoidance, we both ended up succumbing to the virus. It was a great reminder that the smallest of things can stop us in our tracks, make huge differences to our lives, concentrate our minds and push us out of our comfort zones. Friends and family support was so, so essential and welcomed. I am very much more optimistic for 2022.

This new collection has a multitude of themes and ideas running through it but once again, all are of appreciation for love and life.

There is a whole section, towards the back, written in a condensed format, called acrostic. Here the poems body of text literally hangs on the backbone created by a meaningful word or phrase, written down the page. I was learning, through the work of a very wise teacher, how to look for and find grace through gratitude, along with others in our online group, supported by Lisa Davies. This selection includes some of the daily 'thoughts' and my interpretation of them.

I have ventured into writing some verses in the highly distilled, haiku format (named after a Japanese discipline using very limited syllables). I trust you will receive these with kindness, along with all the other verses, in this, my second collection, "Travel Safely Within".

A volume of poetry is like a set of short stories, each a separate entity, with a different tale, character and energy.

Like a box of chocolates, you may find one or two poems are firm favourites but I invite you to give them all a try. Perhaps, by allowing yourself to "Travel Safely Within" your mind, you might feel the words within your heart.

# Memory

A wisp-like presence floats across my mind.

The distant echo of a sound unheard.

Quiet notions of thoughts not said.

A lace-wing touch that was so fleeting.

Why memory, why now do you rise?

# A New Day, A New Start

Awake, awake, a brand-new day is dawning!
There's a fresh start, a clean slate, every morning.
Beginning life with the sunlight once more,
Many choices await you, just unlock the door.

Rouse yourself now, be interested, be keen.
Today is a day you've never, ever seen.
How will you use it, the many hours to fill?
Could you find your true self, by just being still?

Sparkly and novel, many minutes lay ahead,
You've a canvas that's blank, so get up out of bed.
The Universe has sent a time-nugget of gold,
So be mindful of not putting your prime life on hold.

No one else can live this raw day you are given.
The energy rises, an unknown path to be driven.
Be clear of your dreams and see your life's story,
The finishing-line ribbon and the trophy of glory.

Take some deep breaths now, of the cool, crisp fresh air,
Have a shower, scrub teeth, and comb out your clean
hair.
Make good on your promises, refresh any old ways,
Today is the start to the rest of your days.

# Creature Comforts

Could you plump up the cushions?
I'd like to sleep a while more.
Perhaps leave out a snack
In case my stomach should roar?

Maybe add a few logs to the fire that is low?
The warmth soothes my bones, as I snooze in its glow?

My mate's out on the tiles and he's not often wrong,
It's so cold outside, I doubt he will be that long.
Tomorrow there is nowhere that I need be,
So please leave the cat flap wide open, for me.

# Snow Play

A sprinkling of flakes comes down from a sky
That's full with strange clouds bringing more.
It sits just like icing sugar covering the grass,
Trees and tiled roofs just over the road.

Silence descends as it falls without any fuss
But the snow is not driven or deep.
We feel our hearts hasten, in anticipation,
Our inner 'child' wants to get out and play.

It's magical to watch youngsters running outside
With wistful shouts of glee and surprise,
But adults just imagine the places, where later,
We might possibly make snow angels or men.

# Hoar Frost

Right into the bones of the earth you reach.
Fingers of a harsh, cold winter night,
Taking any warmth out of the shallow ground,
Leaving black ice to slip and to slide.

The birds are out waiting for seeds and meal bugs,
Yesterday's are lost way under the frost.
They sing out so sweetly despite being cold,
Feathers fluffed up to just keep alive.

Car windscreens need a scrape before going out
To collect much needed fresh fruit and veg.
The gritters have been but it's much too icy
For them to drive onto small roads like ours.

We put on our layers, adding much needed scarves.
The sun is unlikely to be rising that high
In the metal grey sky that promises little, so
We get quickly onto our tasks to be done.

The ice has set solid in dips, and it groans
As we try it for our weight carefully.
Puddles, now ice rinks on black pavements
But they'll return when the hoar frost retreats.

Hardy walkers pick their way down the path,
Their dogs need their morning trip too.
We wave a hello to the ones that we know
Even though we're not able to shout.

The square is salted and much easier to tread
But it's so quiet with few folk about.
Getting all our provisions, we head back to base
So we can huddle in warmth by the fire.

# Golden Thread

Choosing colours from the rainbow of skeins,
A palette brimming with beauty and promise.
The beautiful design has amazing details
Demanding hours of eye-straining work.

The needle might prick, bringing blood that could stain,
A thimble protects pure white canvas and skin.
Adding the textured design takes pure inspiration.
Taut stitches, with coloured thread, up and down.

Crafters' skills include patience and dexterity,
With good light and time in abundance.
A gold thread will be added to create highlights
Which catch the sunshine when it becomes framed.

The work, when completed will be sent to another,
A friendly tribute and gift from the heart.
Again, the colours and scissors will be tidied away,
Break before another beauty of work will begin.

It's said there's a golden thread between all of us,
Connecting our lives, hopes, thoughts and dreams.
If this is the case, then perhaps stitchers hold a key
To reveal the Universe and all our true mission.

# Friend

You have always been there,

I'm so grateful you care.

When I call you there's no hesitation.

Giving your time to just listen,

As tears fall and glisten,

My lost words tumble out and just fall.

You make all the right noises,

As I fight inner voices,

Deep down in my own troubled mind.

Great wisdom you impart,

As I slowly open my heart,

Full of terrors and questioning doubt.

Holding on to my hand,

You so clearly understand

The drama that's playing out in my head.

Soon we are talking in turn

Of things that we yearn

To share and experience together.

It may be hours that we talk,

We might go for a short walk

But my life seems to brighten with you.

Please accept these thanks, dear,

Knowing I'm always near,

To support you, my friend, as you do, me.

# Footprints

Following footprints made in the snow,
Little wellies, big boots, where do they go?

Following paw prints deep in the snow,
Crossing over grass that's impossible to mow.

Following clear hoof prints cut in the snow,
I would never think there could be a young doe.

Following some claw prints scratched in the snow,
Blackbirds & robins finding plump seeds there, I know.

Following white footprints I make in the snow,
Who might be wondering where I plan to go?

# My Valentine

Well before the day we said, "I do",
I knew I'd always be in love with you.
We hit it off right from the start,
You made me laugh and melted my heart.

In lockdown times we've been confined
And felt we'd maybe lose our minds.
These past twelve months we've spent together
Might have broken an otherwise delicate tether.

Remember, always, to talk, clear the air,
After all, we know we will both be there.
Support and guidance, advice and facts
Exchanged as freely as all of the laughs!

Through all our lives and our endeavours,
My heart is yours, now and forever.

# Orange

How wonderful this fruit is with its deep orange glow,
Shining out bright from the top of the bowl.
Bringing in sunshine to the dimly lit room,
Lifting our mood in the cold, wintry gloom.

The near round fruit, with a cool, waxy skin,
I can feel the dimples coming out and going in.
Brought up to my nose, an instinct so old,
The tangy scent of blossom, that still remains bold.

Turning it in my hands, too good to resist,
My nails dig in deep, the peel hisses with mist.
Sweet, perfumed oil is released from the zest,
Promising the taste of citrus, once undressed.

As the rind comes away in one long, twisty bit,
A smile of delight comes quick to my lips.
I can now see the segments of fruity goodness,
Under veils of thin membrane, just like a promise.

So tempted to taste, I put a piece on my tongue,
The juice escapes easily, taste buds overrun.
Such exotic delights fill my senses with scent,
These moments of eating seem so very indulgent.

The super fresh bits easily pop into my mouth,
So wonderful and tangy, without any doubt.
How fortunate I am that there are no pips hid inside,
I can enjoy this whole fruit, full of natural sunshine.

# Old Orchard

We're both quieter today,
More subdued so less talk.
We head out regardless
For our daily street walk.

The houses are familiar,
With gardens asleep.
Snow's only just melting,
So the puddles are deep.

A route we can take,
Through the old village ways,
Brings us back round, full circle
As on many other cold days.

The old orchard now hosts
A truly wonderful scene.
Every springtime, the locals
Will ask if you've been.

Pass by the old hedgerow,
Full of holly and hawthorn.
Under old, gnarly apple trees
There's an unusual lawn.

A vast swathe of white,
Spikes of such lovely fresh green,
A whole host of snowdrops.
It just has to be seen!

With heads bowed so shy,
They're a heart-warming sight.
A seasonal treasure,
Full of joy and so bright.

We turn to each other,
A smile creeps to our lips.
Natural wonder, once again
Lifts our mood when it dips.

In March snowdrops fade,
Their modest blooms wilt and die.
Primroses will flower here,
To really cheer passers-by.

Another month passes.
We may still walk the streets
But the old orchard trees
Will be in blossom themselves.
What a treat!

# A Welcome Walk

The path may be icy or covered in snow
But I need to get out, move, that I do know.
There will likely be puddles or deep, muddy grooves
Though out in the fresh air, cobwebs I can remove.

The sky is more promising, with patches of blue,
Behind clouds that are fluffy, the sun may shine through.
I get into my coat and don my lovely warm gloves
And set out to walk along streets that I love.

The trees are so wondrous, hard black 'gainst the sky,
Birds cause a rumpus, to and fro, they do fly.
Primroses, crocuses bring yellow and light
To gardens that have had a very long night.

The winter is passing with spring fast on its tail,
Small numbers of daffodils, just peeking out, pale.
The buds on the branches are fuller each day,
Leaves inside poised to unfurl, without much delay.

My trail round the town takes me through the churchyard,
With flagstones set straight, beneath my feet, hard.
I pass by the yew trees and then the lych-gate,
Quite stunningly beautiful, its wood carved ornate.

The market is busy where the Butter Cross stands.

Sunlight warms the skilled work from stone masons'
hands.

The locals chat, catching up with the news,

Of who, what and why before paying their dues.


The walk has renewed both my energy and mood,

I now head for home and make a welcome, warm brew.

The day has turned wet again, with sleety rain showers

But I can rest easy, in our warm home, for hours.

# Spring in the Air

A whisper passes by, held tight on the breeze,
Of what lies ahead but no-one yet sees.
The oceans and Moon work together, with tides,
Once more the high waves, we land-lubbers, must bide.

Gulls drift vaguely landward to capture their prey
But are quite unprepared to find ice in the way.
The freshwater lakes that they usually fish
Are turned into ice rinks, so they skate and just wish.

Milder days follow swiftly, brought in on that breeze,
Moving the branches so bare upon very tall trees.
Days now beginning to lengthen in hours,
With sunrises peachy, red sunsets behind clouds.

The Sun, though it's shy, does its work on the Earth,
Bringing much needed warmth for Nature's rebirth.
That wind passes through, heading possibly west,
A new growing season brings out mice from their nest.

Tender shoots now, are showing above the dark soil.
All winter the bulbs have held back but now toil.
We'll be so happy to see them in colourful bloom,
The new season of spring will be here very soon.

# Moods of the Sea

So inviting and calm,
Tempting and playful,
Boisterous but wistful,
The waves come in, then wane.

Soon churning, oh so dangerous,
Murderous and dark,
Towering, crashing waves
Seem deep, angry and fitful.

Now all brown and muddy,
Murk dragged up with the sand.
Tide changes, now receding
Back to tall breakers again.

Silver and golden highlights
Atop the waves as they foam,
Azure, turquoise and emerald
Then indigo as night and storm falls.

Reflections clear in the shallows.
Peaceful hours on the shore,
Now restful, even meditative
Exchanging restorative thoughts.

# Something Abstract

Stood in the same room, not two feet away
We look at the artwork and both quickly say,
"I don't see the focus, it's all a bit blurred.
What do you see? It all seems mighty queer,
Are you sure it is something, the title's not clear?"

There are colours aplenty, as lines shape a scene
But try as I might, the picture's not what it seems.
I'm at a loss, feeling not just a teeny bit mean as
My friend now makes noises and moves around more.
She's making connections with that work on the wall.

The artist has worked hard, giving all to this piece,
With bright paints and charcoal he has found his true
peace.
I am inclined to move on to the next gallery room,
With further pictures of still life and bold imagery.
Perhaps there is a gift shop or room to have tea?

As I change out the angle, my view opens up.
There, yes there, on the wall, is a giant teacup!
With a beautiful pattern on handle and rim,
How could I have missed this, maybe trying too hard?
At last, I can relax and maybe buy the postcard.

# Up Close

Look up close and it's enlightening.

Move in just so -

You'll be amazed.

Focus on tiny objects.

See how they show

A whole lot of details

You might never have known.


Be up close but leave space to move.

Cramped into corners,

Little room to turn.

Up too tight, feeling

Pushed and restricted.

Allow a safety margin

And scope to rebound.


Get up close and your loved one will smile.

Join the intimate space,

Be welcomed and embrace.

Your breath shares theirs.

Warm skin, tender touch,

Pure energy and heartbeats

Between souls can now merge.

# Art of Light

Walking up to the hallowed, historic building,
I am struck by its Goliath proportions,
Its awesome monumental stonework
Foreboding, magnificent, tall against the sky.
Carved lintels and gargoyles surround frames
Of quarried, dressed and weathered stone.

The windows appear dark, dirty and gloomy,
Slowly approaching the entrance in anticipation.
The door is carved oak, with iron pips to strengthen
Against wind, storms and rain through the years.
A creak on the ancient hinge follows the rat-tat of latch,
With a wide arc it swings open to reveal a cooler inside.

Initially blind after the bright, outdoor sun,
Moving into the gloom lined in hardy gritstone,
The space opens up to cathedral height
As columns and buttresses splay overhead.
Light streams through the myriad of picture panels
Made of handcrafted lead and chinked, coloured glass.

The rose window is such that it steals my breath.
Colour combinations intoxicating, lit up by the sun
Streaming down as if rays came direct from heaven.
Hundreds of years have passed since the men
Turned old stories and shapes of natural wonders
Into this miraculous beauty we can revere today.

# Water of Life

Rain falls on hills, high above where we live.
The rock repels and rejects the cool drops.
Snow might form over cold nights on the peak,
Only to melt and flow down steep terrain.

A bubble of hope eases out of the earth,
Grass surrounding the sodden wet ground.
The wonder that is a fresh mountain spring
Hides in the mud under verdant, green moss.

As the ground slopes away, the water creeps down.
A tiny, wee brook forms there now.
The wonder of life for all beings downstream
Coming forth from beneath solid rock.

An ease through the meadow and wider it flows.
Cattle grazing beside take refreshment.
Flowing deeper, without effort as nature intended,
Muddy bank slopes allowing access for all.

A small lake is seen, caught 'twixt sides of a valley,
The water is cool, peaty and clear.
Fish playfully leap to catch bugs on the breeze
And birds scoop in to float and rest up.

We take from the lake to drink, wash and fuel
The life we have made down the valley.
There always seems plenty but we need to take care
And not abuse nature's generous provision.

The water of life is for all creatures on Earth,
It's not just for man to possess.
We should value highly all things that are living,
And be grateful for the water of life.

# Black & White

Could you be wrong, are you quite right?
The words on the page are bold, black on white.
They tell of your story; it seems to be clear
But is there some grey in which you disappear?

Today meets the future, today leaves the past,
The moment of Now is quickly out of your grasp.
You could feel far too hot and then be so cold,
Ideal warmth between seems so tricky to hold.

Your nib is now blunt, scratching harsh on the page,
Its use is diminished, retired in this age.
A bright light is needed, to craft in your art.
The candle wick burns down, leaving you in the dark.

Day becomes night, the sun slowly it sets,
But the beautiful sky-scene makes your loving heart
melt.
A new day will dawn, a fresh start to present,
Yesterday's words are still there, unless you dissent.

Your mood could be happy, you could also be sad,
Life's never all hilly and rarely all flat.
With storms ever present, we hold peace in our arms,
After writing it down, we might truly find calm.

# Going Out Again

Where should I go? Who could I see?
What is really now expected of me?


We've been in lockdown since this time last year.
Friends and folk are now just starting to re-appear.


It's been oh so long since I dressed to go out,
My mind's in a flap,
Not just what to wear is in doubt.


The truth is not good, I'm not feeling quite right,
It'll take me a while to adjust to 'alright'.


Well, the sky is so blue, the weather is kind,
If only I could quieten this wild, monkey mind.


It's okay to meet, they'd have us believe,
In groups up to six but still no hugs to receive.


Our families can travel to an outdoor venue,
To swap birthday presents now a year overdue.


So I choose a fave top and comb through my long hair,
Then step out in the World,
A true challenge, like Dare.

# Pure Gold

Take a step forward, move into the light,
Your future will reveal itself,
You are destined to shine bright.

You're unsure, just now, of what you will become
But the path is decided and
You shall safely come home.

The beauty and gifts you bring inside your heart
Could truly be more precious than gold.
Words, actions, deeds are waiting, be bold.

Strength to pursue your life's purpose is true.
So softly close your wide eyes and
The way will become clearer to you.

The heart knows the ultimate tests you will meet,
So be trustful and strive ever onward,
Your demons you'll boldly defeat.

Trials will be set for you to perform.
Why, fire maketh man but purifies gold!
Do not allow fear to quash the dreams in your head.

No! Go!
Take that step forward and fulfil them instead.
*Dedicated to Ivar Lewis born April 2021*

# Snow in April

The white blossom petals now rest deep on the ground.
A storm in the night brought us high winds all round.
Now snowflakes are falling, yes, down from the sky
But it's not cold enough for them to remain and to lie.

The squirrel pair scuttle to the feeder with nuts,
Fill their bellies and mouths 'til their cheek pouches jut.
A robin finds grubs in the fly-through affair
Goldfinches squabble, high-pitched tweets fill the air.

Our cats have their breakfast presented on plates.
They don't have to hunt for food or fight with their mates.
A good lick and wash of their fur should suffice
Before sleeping all day, maybe dreaming of mice.

If you listen in closely, you'll hear the bees hum,
Probing for nectar in flowers, pollen coating their bum.
Blackbirds queue for a chance to get seeds for their
young,
With sunshine now bright, spring really has sprung.

# Dandelions

The bright yellow contrasts with the swathe of spring green,

A fabulous crop of dandelions, a delight to be seen.

Some might think of these as nothing, useless weeds

But the bees take sweet nectar and then come the fairy seeds.


The tender leaves are serrated, taken by some as a salad,

Full of goodness, vitamins, iron and fibre to be had.

But the old wives' tales might warn you not to partake

As wetting the bed is a side effect they might make.


In the wild, open verges and hedgerows they grow

But not favoured with gardeners, with green lawns to mow.

It's worth leaving dandelions whilst the flowers do bloom,

There's plenty of time to tidy flower beds and make room.

## Feed Your Soul

Feed your body

Every day, with

Exactly the goodness it

Deserves and desires.

Your instinctive appetite

Orchestrates the ideal food choices for

Use in healing,

Recovery and rejuvenation.

Soul food deeply nourishes and

Offers the whole body an

Ultimate resource for energy

Liveliness and longevity.

## Celebrate with Dance

Celebrate

Every

Living moment with music.

Every musical

Beat

Resonates with

A deeper, instinctive and

Truer

Energy.

With the melody,

It reaches out and

Touches your

Heart.

Dance

Along because

No-one else

Can possibly feel your

Energy.

# Moving On

My sleep is disturbed as the harsh wind it blows.
Rain dashes and drives against fragile windows.
Dreams seem so full of great, night terrors and fears
As I wake with my pillow, dampened with tears.

Such a deep-seated pain, affecting my sight,
Tells of lessons to learn, as if I just might
Not understand, truly, my need to move on
And see that my time in this life phase is done.

I have come across people at all stages in life.
Connections, supporters who've helped through my strife.
Not everyone will stay by me the whole journey long
And expecting no change, in my life-pack, is wrong.

Now awake, the next period of my life has begun.
There'll be days cold with rain or more with warm sun.
I don't know what I'm to do or to which places I'll go
But the people I meet will surely help me to grow.

# Shadows

The shadows always seem a good place to hide,
Strangled light holds fast, disguises all.
No one can see you there, if you are shy,
Enabling you to feel safe, behind your wall.

Dappled rays pick up your shape and form.
Gold splatters bright against the ground,
Under the safeguard of branches high but
Movement gives you away, the faintest of sounds.

It's time to let the sun's warmth touch your skin,
To find yourself in a bright, new day of life.
The darkness will hold onto those deep concerns,
So face-up square to your worries and strife.

The shadows always seem a good place to hide
Away from the spotlight, in your very own night.
No one can see you there, if you are shy
But the World is missing you, shining so bright.

# Riverside Meadow

With beautiful blue skies and sunshine above.
We walk across fields, just taking our time.
The hedgerows are much greener, noisy birds within
And the scent of cow parsley is quite heady, like gin.

Hawthorn trunks bulked out by many years of growth,
The ancient tree boundaries that have thrived in the sun.
Oak, beech and ash add their dimension and leaves,
All different and bountiful, now that summer is here.

Birds startled from feeding their young do take flight
And make lots of noise to distract as we pass.
The fields are now filling with short wheat and corn,
Furrowed deep in the rich earth, our path is well worn.

A riverside meadow, rich in lush grass and clover,
Buttercups strewn like confetti, delicate, so bright.
Inside their gold heads they shine glossy, reflect
The warmth of the sunshine, our chins just deflect.

Sounds of grazing cattle mix with families' fun in the sun.
Swimmers braving currents, freezing water, moods cool.
We pause by the weir torrent, observe boats in the lock
Before heading off home to partake of gin o'clock.

43

# Alone?

Listening, as the clock ticks and the heating hums.

I hear an easterly wind blow and traffic drones by on the road.

A rain shower ends and birds dance on the roof.

I am not lonely, I am alone.


Planes leave their jet streams high above, across the blue.

Thoughts go around in my head, moving like clouds,

Some grey, some white in a huge internal sky of possibility.

I am not lonely, just alone.


My body, once tight now moves freely, like warm fluid.

I stretch, reaching up and out so wide,

Seeing the flexibility of choices for my whole day ahead.

I am not lonely, I am just alone.


A shelf holds a photo of my love and I, on a past sunny day.

We framed it to remind us of how fortunate we are.

I can now look on it, fondly, every single day.

I am not lonely, just have time on my own.

Today I feel emotionally open and look up at clear skies
Through a window of cool glass, framed in white.
I take time for a walk to fill my lungs with clean, fresh air.
I am not lonely, only with time alone.

The beauty of nature surrounds me as I pace along
On my path, hearing the birds sing loud their call.
How wonderful to be able to appreciate it all.
I am not lonely, I am just alone.

# To The Many

Some walked, others marched.
Some flew high but all held heads high with pride
In serving their country, for you and I,
With time and honour, prepared to die.

They stood tall or lay close to the ground,
Perhaps seeking cover on desolate land.
Our thoughts may just wonder
From these carved stones to the sky
And search in our hearts for an answer to, "why?"

Some triumphed one day only to fall on the next.
Comrades that always supported their besties.
All manner of tasks and professions are here
Listed, marked, crests carved and colours appear.

So many to remember, are labelled and named.
Monuments, plinths, sculptures and beautiful trees,
With branches outstretched, to those who strived hard.
To all men, women and children, nature offers a hand,
For paying the ultimate price, to bring peace to our land.

*Inspired by visit to the National Memorial Arboretum*

# Dancing with Dragonflies

A flash of pearly silver flits out before me,

The streak of rainbow colours, a wonder to see.

Iridescent wisps against the open blue sky,

Turn at speed to navigate, wings flutter by.

A shimmer of pure energy dances by me, in sight

Before darting over the hedgerow, a true delight.

# Festival

Another small step back to normality,
An experiment and challenge for me,
In the market there is a book festival
By the magnificence of Newark Town Hall.
Round a corner from church bells that chime,
Just a meander from canal bank and castle,
An observer might wonder what's special
About the square full of folk, with a smile.

Vendors have used lots of fun ribbon bunting,
People are bustling round colourful stalls.
Artistic folk have spread out their quirky
And inspired, eclectic goods for the crowd.
Small children are excited with new books,
Lots of bright pictures, just peachy, the covers.
It's a joy to observe simple happiness,
All the story tellers, authors with smiles.

Young adults and parents are mingling,
Talking words, plots and stories anew.
Love stories, dark thrillers or travel,
They really have all you need, books do.
You can escape into pages of magic
From a world that seems scary, some feel.
There's at least one book here, for everyone,
Not forgetting a page turner and good deals.


It's a delight to be sociable - out again,
Sharing chatter and uplifting exchanges.
A music duo tunes up, now there's singing,
Nostalgic songs filled with hope - nothing changes.
The rain has held off, the sun came out bright,
I've enjoyed some success at my first festival.
Stowing away stock from the stall early evening,
I thank people whose words made up this "thing".

*Created using words 'donated' by visitors to my stall at Newark Book Festival July 2021*

# Look Up

Look up now, look outward, feet forward and true.
The whole world is out there, just waiting for you.
Go see and experience every little detail,
Life is only so long and there's no Holy Grail.

Look up and away from your feet and device,
Let your eyes see, allowing your head to just rise.
Amazing sights will astound you, if given a chance.
Find love in your world, play some music and dance.

Look up and you'll notice all the others here too.
Many looking down, or inside themselves, like you.
All missing so much by not opening their gaze,
Wasting valuable minutes, so many hours and days.

Look up, feel your neck straighten, lift your chin up.
Your entire mood could change, you could refill your cup.
Lungs open, legs stride and your spine can unwind,
A smile on your lips as kind thoughts come to mind.

Look up and you see your own path is now clear.
Twists and turns much less likely to suddenly appear.
Your footsteps can take on a deliberate pace
As you let the sun shining up there, brighten your face.

Look up, know and trust that your feet, they will find,
The true path for you, leave your old past behind.
Your posture has grace now, your future is there,
Take time to tread surely, to heal and repair.

*Inspired by an elderly woman bowed heavily
over a walking frame and younger folk peering into their
mobile devices, all whilst trying to navigate busy
pavements.*

# Stepping into Autumn

Summer has just slipped away, much too easily.
Only yesterday, well it does seem to me,
I was out grounding, barefoot, on green grass
Or out in loose sandals, fresh air my toes passed.

Already I am checking stocks in my tidy sock drawer
And searching for my cosy, warm slippers too.
Ooh, will all my lace-up shoes need cleaning
Or those fluffy-lined boots need heeling?

My feet have worked hard, walking this summer.
They are kept tidy and have supple, tanned skin.
To hide them away yet just seems a huge crime
But needing to stay warm and dry…now's the time.

Oh, in bamboo socks, I have choice aplenty.
Thick, fleece boot liners may need replacing.
Coloured tights to brighten short days now appeal,
Maybe a trip into town would find me a good deal.

I shall now pack away all my open-toed shoes,
Making sure they don't need chucking out.
But as soon as the earth warms and days are longer,
I'll be ready to show my feet again the fresh air.

Stepping out now, there'll soon be a hoar frost
But today there's just dew all around.
Hours of daylight are sure getting shorter
So cosy toes by the fireside I must nurture.

# Letter to the Oak

You stand so tall above me,
I can feel your mighty size.
Your trunk is wide as can be
With branches outstretched, all sides.

I look up, through your crown spreading
Out to capture any light and heat.
I can enjoy shade from leaves a-dappling
On the cool, mossy grass that's beneath.

Deep incisions in characterful bark
Protect a living, wise soul stood inside.
Whenever feeling I am lost in the dark,
Touching you brings me back to alright.

You've lived through so many centuries,
Witnessed events of animal & man.
Would you give up some of the stories
As I palm you, gently, with my hand?

Your leaves, shape distinct, will soon fall,
As the autumn nights, they come down cold.
Each leaf browning is as individual
As are the age-old tales within, you hold.

Perhaps those leaves, all together,
Could make up the pages of your book?
Now so crisp with curled up edges
As the acorns ripen gold in their cups.

Your seeds are thrown down to the ground.
Some squirrels, they take as they find
But the others are spread all around
And send roots, for a new life, down to mine.

Let the beauty of this master oak be known,
It comes not from the roots deep or it's leaf
But lo, it's well-known, charming shadow
On the dusk horizon, dark, in relief.

# Autumn

Autumn has arrived.

Shorter days and cooler nights.

Leaves fall all around.

## Autumn Leaves

Autumn, with its colder nights and

Unsettled weather,

Turns the landscape to

Umber, sienna and gold.

Magnificent trees display their coloured

Nutrients.

Leaves taken by blustery winds,

Every branch is stripped bare

As the ground is covered,

Very lavishly, with the

Exclusive new carpet for this

Season.

# Mist

Mist lingers in fields;

Rich dirt, ploughed deep, sewn anew.

Dawn rises once more.

## Morning Mist

The strange veil hangs low over the fields,

Like a blanket, smothering the land.

The sky overhead is almost clear,

A barely blank page,

With just streams of wispy cloud catching

The early, warm rays of the sun.

Once more, the golden orb rises up,

Into the mauve tints of morning.

It begins…

Another new, crisp bright day for autumn.

## Homelessness

Homelessness

Often

Means that through

Every

Long, seemingly

Endless night,

Sleep is without

Security and another human is in

Need of

Empathy much more than

Silent

Superiority.

*The sad, continuing plight of rough sleepers*

## Ancient Standing Stone

One of four remains,

Holding truth, ancient wisdom,

History stands, still.

# Falkirk Wheel

Unlike in any Venice I know,
Huge gondolas move through the air.
Steel-hulled boats and water, both lifted,
With weightless, graceful ease,
To a higher channel for onward travel.

Through the steel and concrete ribs, like a whale,
Transported into a close tunnel of light.
Slowly, engine pulsing, water parting,
Beneath the ancient fortress remains,
Above much deeper, well-worked mines.

This engineered junction, so well-conceived
Between old cargo routes of industrial times,
Left to falter and fill with silt and reeds,
Now brings fresh life to these waterways,
Old and new ecosystems, coming alive, together.

# William Wallace Tribute

Celebrate freedom,

Honour truth with open hearts.

Treasure loyalty.

*Inspired by an inscription of Loyalty & Liberty*

# Standing Out Proud

There, standing out proud.

Golden leaves, they shout out, loud.

"Not just green, see me!"

# Sense of Memory

The faintest notion of your sweet touch is
Held close in the small space once between us.
Velveteen skin against a warm, silky palm and
Thoughts return to all those tender times.

The faintest of bells chime in the distance.
Dry leaves move in the calm of a breeze.
Waves ebb gently as they reach the shore,
Quietly in and out like your slow, sleepy breath.

Aware of a notion of scent in the air,
I turn my head but you're no longer there.
The sea brings its salt and seaweed tang
But you, my love, only memories bring.

On my lips your taste stayed a good wee while,
Long after our kiss as we parted.
I close my eyes so I can be sure to secure
The wonder that's always been there, between us.

Eyelids shade the sun but I can clearly see
The light of our joy, deep within my heart.
Brightness and smiles still so plentiful
They give succour as the new day arrives.
*Dedicated to Alex for those times apart*

# I Miss the Sea!

Oh, how I miss the sea!

The cool, fresh breeze and salty air.

Gulls crying and weaving

Overhead,

In the blue tinted light,

As they tease and show off their flight.


Oh, how I miss the sea!

The ebb and flow of moon-led tides.

Waves crashing and gushing

Over rocks,

As brine pools reflect light,

The water refreshed through the night.


Oh, how I miss the sea!

The smooth, clean beach below tide line.

Sea washing and healing,

Over time,

My soul, it just might

Find peace, new horizon in sight.

## Create

Create chaos

Create mayhem

Create noise

Create harmony

Create music

Create light

Create fire

Create art

Create design

Create fashion

Create aromas

Create appetites

Create bakes

Create tastes

Create satisfaction

Create space

Create beauty

Create calm

Create peace

Create happiness

Go!

Just create...your very own heart's thing.

Create Love.

# Wake Up

Wake up, wake up, I've brought you a drink.

The spoon on the saucer rattles & clinks.

I know you were out late but you must surely get up?

There's more where this came from, please empty your cup.


A strong, filtered brew of your favourite coffee.

You always remark that it tastes of toffee.

It's all in the origin, beans and the roast

So I do hope you enjoy it, along with your toast.


There's definitely no scrimping, it's spread thick with butter.

The sourdough is smothered, it's so tasty, you utter.

You'll need to be careful of crumbs made from the wheat

Don't end up in your bed as you break crusts to eat.


The day is so bright, with the sun high in the sky.

White clouds are so high up, just breezing on by.

The working week doesn't start for another whole day,

Why don't we go out wandering and let the dogs off to play?

## Back Singing Together

Back in the room among

A nervous, buzzing

Choir, that is so

Keen to begin.

Singing out gently,

In unison,

New songs and old.

Giving our all to

Intuitive harmonies

Now, as confidence

Grows.

Together, the music

Opens up our voices and with

Gratitude,

Energy, as yet held back,

That is now freed, surges from deep within our

Hearts.

Enthralling, engaging, emotional

Renditions…new favourites now found.

# In Your Head

Want a longer lie-in?
The bed is so cosy and warm.
Why not invite the cats in,
It's barely past dawn?

Maybe think to get dressed?
That fancy top's a new fave.
No need to feel stressed,
For another day it will save.

You could put on the kettle,
Choose a Bourbon or Nice?
Maybe blend up a smoothie
Add greens, lemon and ice?

There's that good novel to read,
If you want a diversion
Into another person's thoughts,
Of an adult persuasion.

You could go out for a walk
In the winter countryside,
Hear the birds cry and talk
Or stay in, by the fireside.

I'll be right by your side
If you'd like me to be.
You might prefer it alone
Or be with company.

You might just be OK
Feeling great on your own.
So why have this chat, everyday,
In your head, all alone?

# Winter Solstice

On winter solstice

The cold, shortest day seems shy,

So greet well the light.

# Reunion

Feeling our long separation, by miles.
We have spent many long days apart.
My love for you has only grown
And now fills up my life and heart.

When we are able to finally meet up,
After covering the distance in hours,
I shall be in tense anticipation
Of a reunion so blessed, just ours.

# Betwixtmas

Yuletide glitter fades.

Time between, enough to breathe,

Fresh, new year beckons.

# Grace Through Gratitude – A Collection

*A whole mini-collection of poems in the concise, acrostic style, where the poems body of text literally hangs on the backbone created by a meaningful phrase, written down the page. These were written 'on- a-day' throughout one month.*

*Inspired by the daily meditations and teachings of the World-renowned teacher, Deepak Chopra, followed by our Gratitude & Abundance social media group.*

*You are invited to read the title of each verse and meditate or just 'sit with it' for a short time and allow thoughts to come into your own mind. You might even come up with your own verse.*

## Open Up to Joy

Open up now, your

Protected,

Embodied

Numbness to the light.

Up your

Potential

To seize all

Opportunities.

Joyful abundance

Overcomes

Yearning.

## Gratitude Through Grace

Gratitude

Really

Acknowledges

Those distractions and

Individual

Thoughts,

Usually

Directed

Elsewhere.

Try

Honestly

Receiving,

Openly, the

Unlimited

Gifts from the Universe, its

Help.

Grace then

Remains as

Acceptance,

Compassion and

Empathy.

## Gladden Your Heart

Gladden, feel the

Laughter.

Acknowledge any

Doubt.

Deepen your

Enquiry

Now.

Your

Opening up

Uncovers your

Reality.

Heart

Energy

Always

Returns to you,

Threefold.

## I Am Bliss

**I**

**A**m

**M**astering

**B**liss.

**L**istening and

**I**ntentionally

**S**oul

**S**earching.

## As Grace Replies, Move Forward

As the

Sun rises,

Grace

Releases

Abundant

Choices for

Endless enquiry.

Replies,

Ever

Plentiful,

Lift

Inner

Expectations.

So share...

Move

On,

Vibrantly and

Energetically,

Forward.

Open up to

Receive the

Wisdom.

Allow yourself the

Reward of

Daydreams.

## True Self Lies Deep

True

Reflection

Uncovers

Emotions held.

Self

Evaluation

Lifts up the

Feeling that

Lies

Inside,

Ever

Silent.

Deep

Echoes

Emerge, ever

Powerful.

# Every Moment is Full of Grace

Every

Valuable

Experience

Reflects in

Your

Moments

Of

Mindfulness.

Each

New

Teaching

Is

Satisfyingly,

Full and

Uplifting.

Let

Love

Of self

Find you.

Grace,

Redeeming

And

Complete, is

Enduring.

## Let Go, Accept and Embrace

**L**et

**E**very

**T**hought

**G**o.

**O**vercome.

**A**ccept that

**C**areful

**C**ontemplation

**E**nforces

**P**ositive

**T**hinking

**A**nd

**N**urture your

**D**reams.

**E**mbrace the

**M**agnitude of

**B**ounty.

**R**evere and

**A**cknowledge

**C**reative

**E**xpansion.

## Thankfulness Brings Health

Thankfulness

Heightens

Appreciation.

New

Knowledge

Forges

Unique

Links.

Nourishing

Energy

Surges through

Self and

Brings

Resilience

In place of

Negativity.

Grace

Supercedes.

Health is

Elevated -

Accentuated by

Love and

True

Humility.

## Reality is Truly Personal

**R**eality

**E**xists,

**A**lways,

**L**ying

**I**nside your

**T**houghts, inside

**Y**ou.

**I**s this

**S**tory, being

**T**ruly

**R**evealed,

**U**niquely and

**L**ovingly,

**Y**ours?

**P**ersonal

**E**xamination

**R**e-ignites the

**S**park

**O**f

**N**atural

**A**ppreciation for

**L**ife.

## Accept Others, Open Flow

Accept,

Connect and

Consider

Everyone with

Positive

Thought.

Others,

Thanked and appreciated,

Honestly, might

Extend a

Reciprocal

Sentiment.

Open your

Pathways of positive

Energy

Now.

Flow of true

Love reveals

Opportunities for

Wonder.

# Nature's Generosity is Complete

Nature's

Abundance

Totally

Underpins your

Reality.

Every

Situation offers a

Generous opportunity.

Each

New

Experience

Requires

Ownership,

Submission and

Infinite

Thanks.

Your life

Is destined to be

Strong and

Complete.

Openness will

Manifest

Peace.

Love will be returned.

Extend

This gift to

Everyone.

## Grace is Divine Love

Grace

Really

Amplifies

Connection; our true

Essence.

It is often

Silent.

Divine love

Is to be

Valued.

In

Nature

Everything is

Love.

Overflowing

Virtue replaces

Ego.

## Appreciate All Things

**A**ppreciate the

**P**lentiful

**P**rovisions you

**R**eceive

**E**very day, with

**C**ontentment.

**I**ndeed,

**A**cknowledge all

**T**hings and events

**E**qually,

**A**ll beauty,

**L**ove and

**L**ife.

**T**hese things can

**H**erald the

**I**mportance of

**N**ature's

**G**ratitude and your

**S**uccess.

# Kindness Replaces Judgement

Kindness

Involves

Not creating

Division and

Not allowing

Ego to be

Superior.

Soft-heartedness

Replaces

Every interaction with

Pure

Love

And

Compassion,

Enabling collective

Strength.

Judgement

Undermines and

Disables

Gratitude and grace.

Examine and reframe,

Mindfully,

Every

Negative

Thought.

## Individuality is Wholeness

Individuality

Necessitates a

Desire to

Identify and

Value our

Individual

Differences.

Understanding and

Aligning our own

Lives will

Inherently reveal our

Truth.

Your generosity

Is your

Soul's purpose.

Wholeness of spirit

Holds up and helps

Others.

Let your

Emotions embrace

Nature and all

Encounters.

See that you are, indeed,

Special.

## True Self Has No Limits

True

Reality is

Unbounded and

Expands, infinitely.

Self

Expression in

Love and life can

Fill all space and

Has potential to

Appear as the

Source of all beauty.

No boundaries

Or

Limits can

Inhibit your

Mind

If you break

Through to your

Source of Being.

## Life is Grace is Life

Life

Inspires and

Frees up

Energy.

Is your

Soul ready?

Grace

Releases

Abundance and

Channels positive

Emotion.

Is your

Spirit open?

Life can be

Impatient and intoxicating;

Fully

Embrace it.

# My Higher Self is Ever Present

My internal

Yarn tells of a

Higher

Intuitive

Guide,

Helping my

Ego quieten and

Revealing my true

Self.

Eternally

Living in the

Fullness of grace

Is

Sobering.

Ever

Visible and

Enduring, acceptance is

Remarkable. Always

Present.

Reaching deep, to

Engage and

Speak internally;

Experiencing a

Natural, calm

Tenderness.

94

## My Inner Light Guides Me

My life of

Yesterdays supports my

Inner,

Natural,

Never-

Ending future and self-

Realisation.

Light that's

Inside me,

Graces me with true

Happiness.

Travelling with

Guides that are

Unselfish, ensures

I am able to

Devote

Every moment,

Supporting

Myself, alongside

Everyone I love.

# Divine Light of Grace is Mine

Divine,

Infinite energy

Vibrations are of love.

Indeed, I

Never need to

Envy others.

Light

Is openly

Gifted and

Honoured

To those

Of a

Faithful nature.

Grace is

Returned in

Abundance within the

Calm created.

Everlasting love

Is

Simply

Mine,

If I

Nobly accept it as

Essential for life.

## Spirit Connects to Soul

Spirits of all your

Past

Interactions in life,

Really help to

Interpret

The Now.

Connect with

Others and

Notice,

Not only their

Energy but the

Contributions

They have gifted.

See, at all levels, that

To

Open up your

Soul, brings

Opportunity to connect with all

Universal

Love and light.

# I Am Whole, Complete, Not Separate

I

Am,

Myself,

Whole but

Have so many

Opportunities and

Limitless options for influences.

External influences.

Complete

Openness enables

Me to

Participate fully in

Life.

Every wonderful

Thing

Exists,

Not to just serve me

Or my desires but

To connect all

Separate, universal

Energy sources.

Personal

Acknowledgement of my

Role here, brings an

Abundance of grace and

Tomorrows, full of

Exciting uniqueness.

## Words Speak Volumes

Words, when written down,

Open possibilities to

Render our thoughts and

Describe our dreams in

Safe seclusion.

Speak

Purposefully onto the paper.

Encourage your inner

Author, full of

Knowledge.

Volumes and pages

Of

Love can now

Unfold,

Manifesting and

Expressing your own, living, true-

Self.

## Wealth is All Abundance

Wealth can be seen

Everywhere.

All feelings,

Living beings,

Things and

Health.

Is more money

Something you would welcome?

Are you in

Lack or always

Looking for "it"?

Abundance is about

Beauty and

Understanding,

Not just

Dealt out in

A hand of cards.

No amount of searching

Can bring all you desire.

Enjoy, the here and now.

## Perfect Health is Vibrant

**P**erfect levels of

**E**nergy

**R**esult

**F**rom

**E**xperiencing

**C**ompassion and positive

**T**hought.

**H**ealth

**E**volves through

**A**ccepting and giving consistent

**L**ove.

**T**he amount of individual

**H**appiness

**I**s not rationed or

**S**elective.

**V**ibrant and

**I**nciteful

**B**ody communication can

**R**ealise

**A**bundant and

**N**ever-ending health, with

**T**ime, in balance.

## Love Your Inner Child

Love can be

Overpowering.

Venture to

Explore

Your inner self.

Open

Up your past and

Reminisce.

Inner, deep memories may

Need to be

Noted, well-aired and

Emotions, whatever felt,

Released.

Childhood

Hopes and dreams may then

Invite renewed self-

Love and personal

Direction for your future.

## Travel Safely Within

Travel can

Raise your level of

Appreciation.

Visiting other places may

Enable your

Love of home to rise.

Safely wander

Around your

Favourite destinations but

Enjoy them whilst just

Listening to

Your breath and heart, deep

Within.

In your

Thoughts and memories,

Happy times are

Included with

No need to even leave home.

# Index by Poem Topic

## Grace Through Gratitude – A Collection

## Haiku

## Inspired Reflections

## Lessons in Life

## Mindful Walks

## Seasonal Splendour

# About The Author

After retiring from her own complementary therapies practice of over 20 years, Sue McFarlane has finally found her creative voice and explores many topics within this work. Born in East Yorkshire, now living in Nottinghamshire with her husband and three rescue cats, Sue enjoys rambling in the countryside, exploring nature, cooking and gardening.

## Other books by Sue McFarlane

**My Words for Living** published by Green Cat Books, March 2021

## Reviews of

# My Words for Living

Sue's writing comes from the heart and her energy & love of life shines through. AL

A thoughtful collection of poems that capture the beauty and emotion of nature, life and love coming from a year of uncertainty that has shown how important it is to appreciate these things.

This book gives generously and bravely what it promises on the front. Sue's loving heart shines through with kindness and respect. SW

A varied book with emphasis on the natural world and the world within ourselves. DN

Using everyday language on topics to which I could relate, I found it easy to visualise & feel what these poems were describing and they helped me to gently transition from work to rest mode. ES

A beautiful collection of poems. Honest and reflective. HH

There is a great deal to like in this book. With an emphasis on imagery from the natural world set in a context of human experience, it succeeds in celebrating life and the appreciation of life. AH

For more information about our books, or to submit a manuscript, please visit
www.green-cat.shop

Printed in Great Britain
by Amazon